HEED!

HEED!

Golden Rules for Mentees

Copyright© 2019 by Femi Abiodun

ISBN: 979-886-349-927-7

Published by: ALPHASAGE

Designed by: Israel Odu +2347032607909

Who is a Mentor?

A mentor is someone who dispenses practical wisdom that provokes mental revolution and personal transformation. Great mentors have zero tolerance for Mediocrity. So, if you don't want your ignorance to be damaged, don't seek for mentorship.

A mentor can be a different thing to different people. Below are some of the names various mentees call their mentors:

Instructor, Facilitator, Master, Clarifier, Supervisor, Educator, Mirror, Ladder, "Father", Teacher, Leader, Feather, Collaborator, Tutor, Transformer, Supporter, Counselor, Guide, Protector, Regulator, Elevator, Incubator, Modulator, Projector, Decorator, Pillar, Destiny Helper, Intercessor, Absorber, Motivator, Cover, Coach, Catalyst and so on.

GOLDEN RULES FOR MENTEES

If you disdain the wisdom of your mentor, you will endure the stupidity of a tormentor.

Your association with your chosen mentor should increase you in wisdom and capacity to think for a positive change. His job is to advise you and whatever you do with the instructions given to you will determine how high and fast you will fly.

Many people despise instruction given to them by their mentors because it is either too simple to be true or too hard to execute. Some mentees have ignored their mentors' advise because of over familiarity. If you have a good mentor and despises his instructions, you are doing so at your own detriment. Mentors want you to serve by instruction but tormentor want to put you under servitude by coercion.

Great mentors are always ready to transfer wisdom but will never force instructions on you!

Learn how to stay in the background until your mentor invites you to the limelight.

Your mentor has made some mistakes in the past and wouldn't want you to replicate his mistakes, Therefore, he doesn't want to expose you during the incubation stage. In other words, he doesn't want to expose you prematurely. He knows the right time to launch you out.

Whilst you are in the background, learn all you can learn, observe how your mentor does his things and emulate him. Keep preparing yourself for the day you will have the opportunity to hit the limelight. Let your mentor launch you out, do not attempt to do so on your own because it may be disastrous.

Great mentors are like mighty men holding bow and arrows. If you allow a mighty man to launch you, you will go fast, far and hit your target. However, you may not move fast if you choose to launch yourself.

Your time of staying in the background is a time of learning and building strong capacity. Do not rush out!. Your mentor has the experience and he surely knows the right time for exposure.

The only thing your mentor owes you is instructions, but you equally owe him your results.

G reat mentor genuinely wants you to succeed. He sees himself as your partner in success and wants to be fully involved in your success story. He can achieve this by giving instructions to you.

The only way you can make him happy is to carry out his instructions and get desired results. He is happy when you do well because your result is a confirmation that he is making huge impact in your life.

Some mentees ignore their mentors' instructions because it's either too simple or cumbersome.

Mentor tells you what to do, how to do it, when to do it and why you must do it. Each time you adhere to his instruction, you will avoid errors, difficulties and ordeal your mentor probably experienced on his path to greatness.

Before you admire the glory of your mentor ask for his story because his success secrets is in his story.

Every great mentor you see today didn't fall from heaven. Don't be carried away by his accomplishments. He has a story (both pleasant and unpleasant). Follow every line of his story and apply them in your own life. Every star has scars at a point in their lives. The journey to greatness is not always rosy.

Never admire him so much that you will copy his mistakes.

Ask questions about what he did to get to where he is today. Do not be so fascinated by the "cake" of his success, ask about the recipe. Questions are diggers of life to uncover wisdom, knowledge, insights, ideas and direction. If you ask questions often, you will swim in the ocean of wisdom. Ask questions! Be inquisitive!

Your mentor's story will inspire, motivate and refine you. Learn to be a good student who doesn't talk too much but learn more through observation.

Your mentor will accelerate your growth but he doesn't have all the answers to your questions.

Mentorship is a journey and not a destination. However, on this journey, mentorship guarantee speed and stability.

Mentorship can change your life, income and career for good.

As you are learning from your mentor, he is also learning. Settle it in your mind that he does not have answers to all your questions. However, he will attend to key questions in your life.

The job of a mentor is not to provide all the answers but to stimulate you to go look for the answers and keep developing yourself.

It is very important to cultivate a habit of connecting to God who has all the answers to all questions.

Never choose a mentor based on emotion. investigate before you invest in that relationship.

A lot of people jump at every "successful" people they come across with and ask them for mentoring. It is very important to do a thorough background check about his personality.

I usually advise people to pray about it so you don't pollute or amputate your destiny.

A great mentor should posses some of these attributes:

- An unquestionable character
- Commitment to a laudable vision
- A large heart to help others
- Impeccable Integrity
- Ability to demonstrate wisdom and knowledge

If you don't carefully choose your mentor, you will fall into the trap of a tormentor!

Mentorship will be of no value to you if you are not ready to grow up.

Growing old is compulsory but growing up is optional and personal. For you to grow up you must be ready to live a sacrificial life. Getting the best from your mentor will place a huge demand on your life.

It will affect the way you eat, sleep, talk, socialize, study and so on. It is not an easy task to be mentored by some people. So if you are not ready to grow up, you will groan working with some mentors. Most mentors are not wicked, they just want you to live a responsible and accountable life.

Getting the best value from mentorship entails paradigm shift, change of mindset, breaking of emotional frames and destroying limiting beliefs.

Learning from a mentor is never convenient, it is hard work.

You are expected to stand on the shoulder of your mentor for a period of time so you can see from afar. Don't start "living" on his shoulder.

J ust like a mother eagle tries to wean and teach the eaglets how to fly just for a short period of time before the eaglet will gain mastery. Never expect your mentor to spoon feed or baby-sit you forever.

He wants you to take responsibility once he has shown you the way to go through his instructions.

This is the hard truth: your mentor is responsible to you but he is not responsible for you!

Life is a product of personal adventures, you must deliberately write your own success story.

Your mentor wants you to replicate his success and even surpass him. However, you must not be too distracted by his accomplishments. You must deliberately catch a vision, run with the vision and set an achievable future projection. You are the author of your own success story not your mentor.

You are very unique and this uniqueness should propel you to chase your own greatness and carve a niche for yourself.

All your mentor can do is to support, guide and counsel you and make sure you succeed in your pursuit.

His job is to shorten your journey to greatness. Don't just study him, understudy him too.

Your relationship with a mentor is to abbreviate your own journey to greatness. A good mentor can teach you in one hour what took him ten years to achieve.

However, it is important to be very sensitive to:
- What he says
- What he wears
- Where he goes
- Who he relates with
- What he does

More importantly, you must pay close attention to:
- What he doesn't say
- What he doesn't wear
- Where he doesn't go
- Who he doesn't relate with
- What he doesn't do

Your mentor's instruction is for the construction of your destiny. Take instruction!

Mentees must trust their mentors and obey them. Adherence to mentor's instruction most time drives mentees out of comfort zone but it is in the best interest of the mentee.

You may feel insulted or belittled because of the instructions given to you but you must be humble enough to obey. Until you see your mentor as an authority figure, you can never get the best from him.

If you follow his instructions diligently, you are guaranteed to achieve greatness and huge success.

Now and again, your mentor will give you instructions that are not comfortable or convenient. Just obey them, this in most cases may be the learning curve or part of the protocol.

*It is rude and absurd to
expect your mentor to pay
the price for your personal
development.*

Consider this conversation between a young man who needs a mentor and a successful business man who is ready to mentor him.

Young man: Hello sir, I need you to mentor me.
A Successful Business Man: I am very busy but will agree to mentor you. As part of my mentoring plan, you will travel with me for a seminar outside the city
Young man: Thank you sir, this is fantastic! Can you send me a ticket?

This is wrong!

You are the one who needs mentoring, and you must strive hard to part with your money and resources if you really mean business. It will get to a stage in mentoring when you will ask your mentor some questions and he will ask you to buy some of his materials; books, VCDs or Cds because he has already answered the questions explicitly in those materials.

Your mentor sees you as a serious mentee when you initiate discussion from a portion of his book , his materials or his lifestyle.

If all you are after is your mentor's cash, the relationship will crash.

This is an account of a mentor:

"A young man wanted me to mentor him, and I delayed my response for some reasons because I wanted to study him. One day, he called to ask for financial help. I had the money, but I told him I will get back to him just to test his loyalty. I wanted to be pretty sure if this guy was after my money or he truly wanted me to mentor him. The day he asked for money was the last time I heard from him."

You will lose the benefits of mentoring and may crash on your way to greatness if all you want is your mentor's money. Mentorship offers what money cannot buy.

I often hear this expression amongst young folks and mentees " I covet his wealth"

Don't focus on the luxury apartment, cars, private jets etc. Ask him what it costs him to acquire these things instead of asking him to give you money to get them. Never beg for money or material thing from your mentor, it is forbidden!

Your mentor may choose to be your sponsor if he wants to but he is not under any obligation to do so.

Set your motive right. Go for knowledge. When you are knowledgeable, money will come your way and you can afford whatever you want to buy.

*Be emotionally intelligent
when dealing with your
mentor. He is not an angel.*

Your mentor is not a superhuman. What attracted you to him are his strengths but never forget that, he has his weaknesses too. It is very important to know that we all have emotions, habits, temperaments, attitudes, idiosyncrasies and so on. It is mandatory for every mentee to carefully study the personality of a mentor very well.

- Some mentors are choleric.
- Some are sanguine.
- Some are phlegmatic.
- Some are melancholy.

You must understand each of them and deal with them accordingly.

The best way to deal with your mentor is to drop your "emotional baggage" so you can get the best out of him.

Have you ever thought that your mentor has his challenges, plights and low moments? Be sensitive at these periods. For instance, if your mentor is bereaved, you should know that you are to commiserate with him and not to ask him to solve problems for you at that point in time.

The best gift you can give to your mentor is your success story.

Your mentor is not only interested in teaching you the principle of greatness, but he also wants you to experience greatness. Mentoring is an investment, and he wants a huge Return on Investment.

As a mentee, you must prove to him that you have not wasted his time (and sometimes resources). Your mentor is earnestly waiting for your success story because it will bring fulfillment to him.

Because he did not charge you for whatever he has done for you, his own reward is your success story.

Every mentor feel the insult when you don't have result.

entors are livid when you don't replicate their achievements. People will appraise you based on your mentor's achievements and if you are not producing results like your mentor, they will likely mock you. The impression this creates is that your mentor has not done a good job, so he feels the insults as well. Just like a students who fails because he did not follow his teacher's instruction to the letter.

Your teacher (who is a mentor) also shares part of the blame and mockery if you fail the examination of life.

You must have it at the back of your mind that most great mentors have zero tolerance for mediocrity and failure especially after they have invested so much in you

Respect your mentor but never worship him. Every king you see today was once a crying baby.

Give your mentor an undiluted respect and honour he deserves but never idolize him. Be careful the way you relate with him so he doesn't take the place of God in your life because in the organogram of life, God is still at the top.

Be cautious in your greetings, ovations, accolades, conversations and be sure you are not worshipping him. Whatever feat your mentor has achieved today is also achievable if you choose to carefully follow his instructions and work harder.

A good mentor will raise you but a bad one will "raze" or "erase" you!

Every record can be broken. Don't be intimidated by the achievements of your mentor.

It is good to admire the accomplishments of your mentor but you must know that every record can be broken. A great mentor will even be happier with you when you break the record he initially set.

Never be intimidated and write yourself off that you cannot beat his record. It is possible. It is achievable but it takes a lot of hard work!

Great mentors pass the baton of greatness to their mentees so they can continue from where they stopped. Therefore, there is an ample opportunities for focused and success-driven mentees to do much better than their mentors.

However, be very careful so you don't start competing with your mentor. If you do so the relationship will break.

The mentor you abandoned like a rag in his dry season will be useful on your rainy day. Always stay connected with your mentor no matter what.

Your mentor is a box of wisdom. A time will come when you will "arrive" and think you don't need him again. It is advisable not to be too far away from your mentor because his wisdom is eternally useful. A lot of people don't keep in touch with their mentors as soon as they become great, no phone call, no checking up on their mentors. They feel they are expired!

You must cultivate the habit of keeping in touch with your mentor always. Sometimes it becomes too late for some folks to get the best from their mentors when they run into trouble that can be easily managed by same mentors. Don't ever think your mentor's intelligence is outdated to solve contemporary problems. Remember, he is still learning, unlearning and relearning and sees education as a lifetime adventure.

You can be more successful than your mentor, but you cannot outgrow him!

Never abuse the privilege given to you by your mentor.

When your mentors allow you to access their private spaces never abuse such privilege. Such privilege is priceless and must be cherished.

For instance, if your mentor gives you his private number, don't think you can call him anytime you like or give his number to anyone without his prior knowledge.

If your mentor introduces you to any of his friends, partner or contact, it is sheer abuse of association and embarrassment to him if you reach out to the person without his prior approval.

Be very cautious by learning to protect, respect and honour privileges given to you by your mentor.

As a matter of fact, when you are with your mentor, listen more and talk less!

Emulate your mentor but never imitate him. You will become the second best when you try to be like someone else.

Some mentees copy everything about their mentors and lose their own identity in the process. They don't plan it but suddenly, they find themselves doing it unconsciously.

They want to talk like him, walk like him, dress like him, eat like him. People will not remember you, they will remember your mentor whom you consistently copy.

You are the original version of yourself, you have your own peculiarities and you are designed for your own purpose.

Imitation makes you so cheap.

You can be mentored by someone who is younger than you are. Age is not a pre-requisite to mentoring.

Age has nothing to do with wisdom, it is just a number. What you need from your mentor is wisdom not age.

The answer to many people's problem lies with someone who is much younger but pride will dissuade them from learning from such person.
They believe they can only be mentored by an older person. It takes humility to submit to a mentor especially your age mate or a
younger one.

A school of thought humorously says that "the old age of Methuselah is less important than the wisdom of Solomon"

If you know anyone who has what you need to succeed in life but far younger than you, get close to him and let him mentor you.

Invest your time wisely with your mentor. He is very busy with his assignment and possibly mentoring other people like you.

One of the key skills you need to have if you want to enjoy mentoring is time management. Whenever you are with your mentor, go straight to the point.

Mentors are always very busy and in most cases, they squeeze out their precious time to attend to your issue. They understand the currency of time and they don't squander it. Don't be a storyteller.

Do all you can to ensure you don't waste his time. If you don't manage his time, you will get him weary or irritated. Eventually, he will avoid you and the relationship may suffer a setback. Don't spend time with your mentor, invest it!

If you really honour your mentor, you will honour his time. Never waste his time for any reason!

You must be sensitive to the "moment of impartation" by staying focused whenever you are with your mentor.

I know some mentors who are very jovial. They talk and crack jokes like comedians. He will crack jokes throughout your discussion but while he was cracking jokes, he has given you a solution to your problem. Many mentees get carried away by the joke and miss that "moment of impartation".

If your mentor is a speaker or teacher or preacher, pay attention to everything he says because he may just have mentioned the solution to a challenge you are dealing with.

You must be very sensitive, focused and be at alert whenever you are talking or walking with your mentor.

Respect protocols. Do not bring anyone into the circle of your mentor without his prior approval.

Protocol is very essential in mentoring. If you truly respect your mentor. It is a taboo to bring another person into the circle of your mentor or disclose confidential information about your mentor without a prior approval from your mentor.

If you keep bringing people to him without a notification, he will no longer trust you and the relationship may end abruptly or on a bad note.

Mentors love their privacy and they don't open their doors to all and sundry. They are very selective in who they allow into their lives. To some mentors, it is a grievous offence to bring strangers to them without prior notice and they can cut off the relationship immediately.

Be guided.

Listening is the major tool you need to get the best from your mentor. Never show off what you know. If you know so much, you don't need mentoring in the first place!

A lot of mentees don't listen to their mentors. They hear him but don't listen to him. You are there to learn not to display your analytical or oratory skills.

Some mentees go to their mentors to display what they know. In all honesty, if you are so full of wisdom then you don't need a mentor!

Listening is a skill every mentee must acquire and develop. Let your mentor do the talking while you do the listening.

Whenever you are with your mentor, listen with rapt attention, I mean listen, listen and listen!

Your *"gifts"* will make
more room for you from
your mentor and will
position you well.

ind a way to appreciate him for choosing to mentor you, it is by privilege. Never abuse the privilege of being mentored, it is not your right.

Buy unsolicited gift for your mentor. He is not after your gift, but you need his wisdom. As a matter of fact, you will enjoy the grace your mentor carries when you continually sow "seeds of appreciation" with the right motive. If your motive for sending him gift is wrong, you will not get the best from him. No mentor is allergic to honour.

Stay loyal to him and recommend him for a position, assignment, project, business that suits his profile whenever such opportunity present itself. This is one of the best gifts you can give to your mentor.

*Clean up your ugly past
and allow your mentor to
write on a clean slate in
your heart.*

Never amplify your past mistakes if you want to get the best from your mentor. He is really not interested in your past. He wants to work on your present so that your future will be secured.

Many mentees are still carrying the heavy baggage of their past lives. This has been a major impediment to follow instructions given to them by their mentors. They are locked up in their minds that it will not work because of their past experiences.

Until there is a shift in paradigm, change of mindset and belief system, the valuable instructions passed to you by your mentor will make no sense to you and will never work for you.

Be mindful of what you say and what you don't say whenever you are with your mentor.

If you are too garrulous, you will miss the value of mentorship. Let your mentor do the talking while you do the listening. Let him take the position of a teacher while you take the position of a student. He has created time for you to groom and develop you. He has no time for gossip, backbiting and idle talks. If all you do is to talk about things that doesn't concern him or outside the scope of mentoring, he will eventually cut you off.

A school of thought says *" a closed mouth is a closed destiny".* Therefore, never close your mouth in any of these situations:

- When you need clarity on a particular subject matter.
- When you have access to information that will help your mentor in any way.
- When there is a danger ahead of him.
- When you can be helpful to him.
- When you need to show appreciation.

You will never be complete, if you choose to compete with your mentor.

When a mentee starts to compete with his mentor, the relationship will eventually crash.

One of the few things that jeopardizes mentor and mentee relationship is competition. Once your mentor sense competition, he may not show you the trade secret. There is no point asking for mentoring if you are not convinced about your mentor's superiority. Being competitive with your mentor is a product of pride.

Competition will make you lose the key benefits of mentoring.

Your mentor's bitter lessons should not be your experience.

In mentoring, a serious mentee is not expected to replicate the errors of his mentor. Most mentors made mistakes while climbing the ladder of greatness, but they don't want their mentees to repeat the same. It will be a major disappointment if you repeat the errors made by your mentor.

Your mentor wants you to follow him closely but never copy his mistakes.

Without loyalty and allegiance, you cannot win the heart of your mentor.

F rankly speaking, every mentor is looking for a loyal mentee. Your mentor is so much interested in your "heart service" and not **"eye service"**.

Your loyalty to your mentor will make your relationship to be more cohesive. Many mentees are only looking for what they can gain from a mentor even at his detriment. The only way you can prove to your mentor that your relationship with him is not for personal gain is to remain loyal to him.

A time will come when "outsiders" will speak ill of your mentor. Never join them to pull your mentor down. You must be able to defend him, don't join the gossip chain. A lot of mentees don't care to bite the fingers that fed them.

At a point when you feel you have outgrown your present mentor, go and look for another mentor before you compromise your full loyalty to him.

The deep secrets of your mentor's success is "caught" not "taught". Be vigilant!

Being vigilant with your mentor is a point we cannot overemphasize. You must be on your guard , most secrets that will transform your destiny are shared when you least expect. If you miss it, it may be very difficult for such moment to happen again.

In this case, your mentor will not teach you but he expects you to catch the eye-opener and run with it. For instance, you mentor may not teach you how he manages his daily routine but you must study him well and emulate. Study the way he relates with his colleagues and family.

You may also need to study him very well how he manages himself during crises and difficult times. There are some things you will see him do but he will never sit you down to teach you, you must be vigilant and catch these things.

Learn to discern between the personality of your mentor and the gift he carries.

Most mentee pay so much attention to the personality and lose focus on the gift he carries.

Some mentees do not like the behaviour of their mentors. What you need is the gift, knowledge and wisdom. Don't be distracted about some of his strict principles.

Focus on the gifts and his wisdom reservoir. Sometimes, he may be too difficult to deal with, just make sure you are learning from him.

Until you allow your mentor to master you, you can not be a master in that field.

Mentors are masters. They understand the terrain where you want to travel on, they understand the velocity at which you should travel. They know the secrets to arrive safely and swiftly. This is why you need a mentor.

Mentoring will provide the direction you need so you can be transformed from being a rookie to a guru. He has done it before and he is currently doing it but you have probably not done it before. You must be humble and learn from the master.

The road to greatness is not smooth, if you know before you go, it is strategy and if you don't know before you go, it can lead to tragedy.

Let your mentor show you how it's done so you won't travel in a wrong direction.

You must honour your mentor because he is one of the few people who truly want you to be great.

A school of thought says "for you to succeed you don't need anyone permission but you need their collaboration". So if your mentor collaborates with you to succeed, never take this for granted.

Mentors are always there to give you the push and the encouragement you need to forge ahead in the quest for success. He pulls you up when others push you down. He is your praise singer when the mockers are there to derail you from getting result. Not everyone wants you to succeed but your mentor provides a solace when you feel like backing out. Every genuine mentor is a fortress.

Mentorship is a journey not a destination, so every mentee must protect, galvanize and promote the relationship so they can do great stuff together.

Your attitude of gratitude will attract great assistance from your mentor.

Remember, mentorship is a privilege not a right. You are very fortunate to be mentored so don't take this for granted.

Show appreciation always. Buy him gift before your scheduled visit, buy him a gift for his birthday, spouse's birthday, wedding anniversary and during festive periods. He will surely appreciate your kind gestures. This shows how much value you place on the relationship.

However, if your mentor solicit for gifts from you, he is a tormentor. Great mentor will never compel you to buy gifts for them.

Smart mentees will never visit their mentors empty-handed. No matter how small, they will present a gift.

Over familiarity with your mentor can be disastrous, beware!

There is huge temptation for mentees to disdain a lot of things about their mentors because of closeness. It is dangerous and even more dangerous when you are dealing with spiritual mentors.

The fact that you see him and follow him closely or you are privy to certain information about him does not give you license to dishonour him or play on his intelligence. Never do anything that will make him get angry or cut off the relationship.

If your mentor doesn't like a particular thing, don't do it because some mentors will never forgive you for taking them for granted. Some may forgive but will never forget. Do study your mentors carefully to know his likes and dislikes.

Always think about how you can support your mentor in fulfilling his dream or achieving his set goals.

Here is a story of a young man who wanted a great man to mentor him. He sought his attention severally, but the man was always very busy. One day, he just asked the man and offered to help him handle his media and recordings? The man said yes and jumped at the offer. Today, this young man is one of the best in his industry because the mentor deliberately taught him the trade secret. He got the best from his mentor because of his giving mentality.

Apart from money, what do you have to give to your mentor to make his life easy?

You must know that your mentor has needs, ambition and dreams. One of the way to display your loyalty to your mentor is to always offer to help him fulfill his aspirations with your talents, skills and time. When you do this continually, he will be more open to you and teach you more things.

If the mentorship adventure is not geared towards your personal transformation. You are dealing with a tormentor.

A great mentor is the one who rebukes, corrects, counsels, advises and instructs. All these must lead to total transformation of the mentee. As a mentee, if the relationship with your supposed mentor doesn't translate to a significant personal transformation or mental revolution, you are probably dealing with a tormentor.

Many are following tormentors, and they think he is a mentor. If you are following anyone who should be a mentor but has any of these traits, then he is a tormentor:

- He doesn't allow you to find your unique voice
- He is intimidated by your vision, ideas, gift, purpose and potentials.
- He doesn't tolerate your mistakes
- He creates little or no time for you
- He doesn't provide you opportunity to grow
- He is very stingy with commendations but generous with destructive criticism
- He always coerce you to give him money or serve him
- He is impatient with you
- He doesn't give you platform to network
- He takes advantage of you, sexually harasses you or amplifies your weaknesses.

Contact FEMI ABIODUN

*To have Femi speak at your conference,
Workshop, School, or Church programme*

Contact
Facebook: *Femi Emmanuel Abiodun*
Instagram: *@femiemmay*
Email: *femiemmay@gmail.com*

Printed in Great Britain
by Amazon

44380155R00050